My Jewish Journey to Christ
A Public Testimony

> *Secretly, I wanted so much to believe. I was so jealous that I was not a part of this wonderful community of believers. Never had I experienced the comfort of belonging as I did at IBC. Even though I had not accepted "their" God I was still accepted by them, as one of them. This stirred jealousy in me and created a sense of loss and separation from the group since I was not able to feel what they felt. I so wanted the Lord to enter my soul and take away the burden, the longing moreover, the emptiness I had lived with most of my life. On the morning of Saturday, January 7, 2007, the Lord sent His Spirit into the depths of my soul. I was finally free. I was finally one with Him, my Savior.*

Revised February 2024

Preface

This book was first published on November 11, 2014. The response has been amazing. Readers have all said they have really enjoyed becoming a part of my life as described in the book. Many older readers have had flashbulb memories when reading about my time in Chicago and my travels around the world. I know many of my readers but never shared my journey with them until the release of my personal testimony.

I have also received many questions from them that I felt needed to be answered and gave me the impetus to write a revision of the original book which I am doing in this publication. I have also added photographs that I believe bring more of a 3rd/4th dimension to my story and gives readers a more personal glimpse into my life. (Due to printing costs, I have chosen to keep these black & white.)

It is my personal hope that you will be both inspired by my journey and to enjoy reading about my many travels in the USA and around the world.

I have done my due diligence to keep my story in chronological order, however some of my stories have had a mind of their own and have landed in various places along the way. I will start in 1960, the year of my birth and end as close to my new publishing date.

There were also many temptations to include parts of my life that were not relative, which I was able NOT to include here. Perhaps a future biography.

"Blessed are You, our God, Ruler of the Universe, who is good and causes good."

Baruch atah Adonai Eloheinu meleḥ ha'olam hatov v'ha'meitiv."

Steven Lee Douglas

Content

In the Beginning	7
Japan 1960	9
A Sour Experience in Venezuela	15
The House on Castlewood Terrace	17
1970's, My Teen Years, Turtleneck Bowling Scandal and Trip Around the World	21
My Grandparents	22
Jewish Traditions	27
Ethical Humanism	31
Judaism: A Nationality, a Religion, or Both?	33
3 Generations of American Levites	39
My K-8 Education	41
My 13th Year – Bar Mitzvah?	45
Visit to Israel and my "True Jewish Awakening."	49
The Highschool Years and My Coming of Age	59
Saved by an Angel	61
Time to Straighten Up	63
My first introduction to the "*God of the Christians*" and Scripture...	73
My First Baptism	75
1980's – My Twenties - College and the University Years – The Lone Jew of Catholic U becomes the Defender of the Jews.	77
1983 – 1990: The Silent Years.	91
The 1990s. My Thirties	93
The Beginning of My Journey to Christ	95
Back in the USA	89
West Virginia and Independent Bible Church	101
Saturday, January 7th, 2007 The Day of my Spiritual Awakening	113
Did I experience an Epiphany?	115

Baptism	117
Prayer – The True Foundation of Faith	119
17 Years Later	123
A Special Thank You!	127
Supplements	
Duties of Priests and Levites (Numbers 18:1-7)	129
What is Hannukah: Festival of Lights	131
Focus on Pastor Randy Bradley	133
My Dreams (Supplemental)	137
Index for Photographs	145

In the Beginning....

I was born April 23, 1960, the son of a Jewish mother and a Jewish father. My parents were not just Jews but were direct descendants of the prophet Aaron the older brother of Moses. According to Torah (Exodus 28:1), part of the law brought down from Mount Sinai by Moses, anointed Aaron the first High Priest of the Israelites, a designation that continued to his male descendants. A designation my parents told me my brother and I received at birth. According to Jewish tradition this designation continues in modern times. Until many years later, I was unaware of what any of this meant.

> Exodus 28:1
> And you bring near to yourself your brother Aaron, and his sons with him, from among the children of Israel to serve Me (as kohanim): Aaron, Nadab; and Abihu, Eleazar, and Itamar. Aaron's sons.

According to modern tradition, the Kohanim have the privilege of being called for the first Aliyah to say the blessing over the Torah during religious services. There is also the privilege of saying the priestly blessing; for Ashkenazi communities, of which my descendants are from in Europe, the Aliyah is only recited on major Jewish holidays. (See the section on the 1990s.)

Japan 1960

At the time of my birth, we were living in a small village outside the city of Okayama, Japan. We had chickens, dogs, and cats. My father was a visiting scholar teaching dentistry, and my mother was teaching English at a local Japanese high school and volunteering her services at a nearby leprosy colony.

My parents had moved to Japan from New York City in late 1958 with my older brother. My family remained in Japan until late 1961 at which time we boarded a ship and sailed back to the USA. I learned later that I was the biggest baby ever born in Okayama Prefecture and was given the nickname of *Momotaro* (Peach Boy), a folk story of a boy born from a peach who was a local hero to the region. It is a wonderful children's story I read to all my children.

Momo Taro

We moved to Berkeley, California in late 1961 where my sister was born in January 1962. After a couple of years in Berkeley we moved to Chicago where my father took a teaching position at the University of Chicago and began his first practice as an oral surgeon.

Our first home in Chicago was a 2nd floor rental apartment overlooking the lakefront, near to Lincoln Park Zoo. This Goethe statue was located close to our apartment building at Diversey Ave and Marine Drive.

It was when we lived there that I suffered my first life stress-event. I mention this because I believe my various life-stress events have been critical to my journey through life. Scott, the older (and self-directed protective) brother of a friend in the building pushed me down a flight of stairs and I broke my leg in two places.

My 2nd stress-event also took place on Lakeview Avenue when my mom was driving our station wagon, and another car came barreling down in the wrong direction and slammed into the front of our car.

I flew from the back seat into the dashboard and lost most of my baby teeth. I remember lots of soft serve vanilla ice cream. No, my mother was not negligent as in those days there were no backseat seatbelts.

The 3rd stress-event (remember everything comes in 3's.) I had in that part of my life was playing darts with my brother in front of the apartment building when he threw a dart into my knee cap. That was minor but one of those flashbulb memories of my early childhood.

In the winter of 1967, we had the Great Chicago Snowstorm. It led to one of the only good memories I had with my dad when we left our brownstone on Lakeview Avenue and walked into Marine Drive in Lakeview Park where cars were stranded in many feet of snow. We brought them coffee and donuts. Stranded drivers were very appreciative.

The Great Chicago Snowstorm

Closer to New Years my parents had purchased our new home on Castlewood Terrace, and we took a trip to South America while a moving company packed our apartment and moved us into our new home.

During our trip to South America, I had the greatest fortune to stay in all-inclusive resorts. At least in those days, there were fruit trees all over the property and my sister and I wasted no time exploring it.

A Sour Experience in Venezuela

I can still remember being able to order anything I wanted at poolside since everything was so cheap and all I had to do was sign for it. If it ever was expensive my father never told me. Aside from the great souvenirs I brought home including the jawbone of a donkey and a dried piranha on a piece of wood, I also learned the important fact that a lemon was not a grapefruit. My sister and I found a large lemon and when we brought it to show to our parents, we insisted it was a grapefruit and to prove our point, we ate it, with lots and lots and lots of sugar.

That was the trip when we took an excursion to a water village called Sinamaica where all the homes were floating above the water on stilts. We also saw a real cock fight where the losing bird had its head twisted off. I was 9. 11.0865°N 71.8544°W.

When we arrived home to Chicago, we found that someone had broken into our new home. My father quickly got an alarm system installed including a direct alarm to the local police department which came in handy later when I needed help...

The House on Castlewood Terrace

In 1969 my parents bought this home on the near-north side in an old neighborhood called "Uptown." For any Chicagoans reading this, we were located at 4800 North between Sheridan Avenue and Marine Drive, two blocks north of Lawrence Ave. A trip to the street is well worth the future memories. Just remember to imagine seeing Charlie Chaplin walking down the street.

Our new home was a beautiful large all-brick home. Castlewood Terrance is only 1 block long and has an incredible history dating back to the beginning of the 20th Century. The 26 homes that make up the street were all originally owned by the producers and stars of the silent film industry.

Our home, at 841 West Castlewood Terrace, was first lived in by actors and newlyweds, Wallace Beery, and Gloria Swanson.

Wallace Beery   Gloria Swanson

The home across the street was first owned by Douglas Fairbanks, Sr. The same house became the future home of Studs & Ida Terkel. Studs was a famous radio personality in Chicago and became a playwright in his later years. I mention this because his wife Ida Terkel became an important part of my life as a trusted friend. I rarely saw Studs because he traveled constantly.

"Studs"

The Keystone Cops

Many do not know that before Hollywood, the film industry started in Chicago. Silent films were the main productions and were filmed at Essenay Studios, which were located no more than a mile from Castlewood Terrace. Although he was not a resident of our street, Charlie Chaplin made many of his films at Essenay Studios. The "Keystone Cops" movies were also filmed there.

1970's, My Teen Years, Turtleneck Bowling Scandal and Trip Around the World...

When we lived on Castlewood Terrace, most of the family were members of family bowling leagues at the Marigold Bowling Lanes. I do not know if it still exists but, in those days, it was a prominent place for the Douglas family. I was pretty good and one year competed in a youth bowling tournament. I won in my local league and again in regionals and ended up in the Illinois State finals in Springfield, IL. Not to gloat (OK, I'm gloating), I was the best in the City of Chicago for my age group.

My 90-year-old mother can still remember to this day what happened in the final game, probably because I reminded her of it for many years after. My mother made me wear a turtleneck shirt. I had a nervous tick in my neck and that turtleneck was like a snake around my neck with itching powder mixed in.

My final score got me 11th place. The first-place score was 30 points below my personal average. I reminded my mother, for many years, of this and even with her short-term memory loss, she never forgot this incident. Admittedly I did remind her quite a few times through the years.

My Grandparents

Just a quick note on my grandparents. My father's father was from the last religious generation of the family. I remember hearing that he occasionally led high holy day services at a small temple in the Flatbush neighborhood of Brooklyn, New York. He was also a practicing oral surgeon and rumor has it he once took an emergency appointment with actor and comedian Bob Hope.

I am not sure why my father did not continue the tradition after having had a Bar Mitzvah. My mother's father died before I was born, and I am not aware of his religious interests. Although the tradition of Aaronides' is through the father, I do not want to forget my favorite grandparent, Rose Schneider, my grandmother, and mom's mother. After her husband Clifford died, she relocated to an apartment building in Old Hollywood, California. She had a swimming pool and I used it many times when I went to visit her. Fortunately, my parents sent me quite a few times to visit her and our California based family. When my mother was younger, although they lived in Brooklyn, they took the train many times to visit their family in California. One of my mom's favorite stories was that she used to visit the home of Lou Costello of the comedy team Abbott and Costello.

Bud Abbot & Lou Costello

In addition to my mom's stories, I was lucky to have my own stories about being in Hollywood. One summer, my parents rented a cabana at the Edgewater Beach Hotel.

The Edgewater Beach Hotel

The cabanas were shared, and we were extra fortunate to share ours with the parents of actor Tony Randall, famous for his role as Felix in the phenomenally successful sitcom, *The Odd Couple.*

Tony Randall

Tony came to visit Chicago during the summer a couple of times, and I remember playing foosball with him and other kids in the pool. Thanks to the cabana connection, I was able to visit Tony when I went to visit my grandmother in Hollywood.

He invited me as his guest to visit Universal Studios where he gave me a personal tour of the sets. I cannot remember anything about the tour other than visiting the cafeteria where the actors ate and personal introductions to two of his acting friends, Telly Savalas (famous for his TV show "Kojak") and Lucille Ball. Telly Savalas was sucking on his iconic chocolate lollipop.

Telly Savalas    Lucille Ball

Entrance to Universal Studios

Jewish Traditions

I think a disclaimer here might make some sense. As in Christianity and Islam, there is more than one sect of Judaism and what I believe are Jewish traditions, may be alike, but also different than others.

With that noted, when our grandparents were alive, they regularly sent us gifts to celebrate Hanukkah. My Grandma Rose included the Hanukkahstory books about the War of the Maccabees, the dreidel game and most importantly Hanukkah Geld (chocolate coins in gold foil)

In my teen years, when my grandmother Rose could, she would send a big holiday box with different gifts to open on the 8 days of celebration. In our home, unless directed by the grandparents, we acted like it was Christmas morning (yes, we celebrated that too, at least the commercial Christmas). My parents certainly knew about Jewish tradition having been brought up in Jewish homes in Brooklyn, but they rarely shared anything with our generation.

My mother was an avid reader and shared what she knew about the history of the lighting of the candles at Hannukah and we always had a Menorah that was lit each night in our home. I don't recall learning the prayer from my parents. This happened when I went to Anshe Emet in Chicago. (see My K-8 Education)

I have never failed to continue this tradition with my kids in my own home. I always have my youngest recite the prayer for the lighting of the candles. As I look back, the customs of the Jewish holidays were always fun when we celebrated them.

Hannukah Menorah

In the springtime, we rarely celebrated the Passover Seder. Jewish holidays were not looked upon with favor by my father, or he just never had time for them. I seem to think that he purposely stayed away from both organized religion and the traditions of Judaism. The only time I can recollect organizing the Passover Seder were in my own home when my two older children were still young enough to keep focused, and later in life when I attended The Catholic University of America and at the Independent Bible Church in Martinsburg, WV, the latter being a Messianic Passover Seder service.

I know my father had a Bar Mitzvah when he was 13, but I have no memory of him *acting* Jewish. As I mentioned earlier, his father was more religious than his son, but we were not remarkably close, and he did not visit Chicago that often from his home in Flatbush, NY. Ironic, the only photograph I have of his father is his Bar Mitzvah picture.

Ethical Humanism

Soon after we moved to our new home in 1970, my parents joined the Ethical Humanist Society of Chicago, in Evanston, IL. The Ethical Humanist Society was made up of members from many social classes and many different faiths. They met on Sunday mornings and had adult fellowship led by their Society leader, and we kids had Sunday school. The leader was able to conduct marriage ceremonies. Compared to churches and temples, it was not that different from other organized religious experiences, but one thing was missing.

Ethical humanists believe that humans control their destiny and lives. They believe that God is a theory created by, and used by, man. They are some of the strongest supporters of the Big Bang theory and Darwinism. The Society's headquarters in Washington DC once had a sign out front that read "We spell God, G-O-O-D." My older brother, younger sister and I were raised by Jewish Ethical Humanist Atheists.

Judaism: A Nationality, a Religion, or Both?

My mother, a self-professed ethical humanist continued to light Hanukkah candles well into her early eighties. She was trying to keep her Jewish tradition alive. Where this gets confusing is that, to this day, she blatantly refuses to accept any possibility that there is a God. Her ethical humanism, which dominates her beliefs, does not allow her to believe in a holy spiritual realm. My mother contends that Judaism is a nationality and that the traditions such as Passover are not religious in nature. Considering that Judaism is formed on the Old Testament. or Torah, and this group of scripture being about God and His chosen people it behooves me to understand how she can separate the two.

She is not alone in the belief that Judaism is a Nationality. When I worked and lived in Russia during the 1990's, one of my best friends was Jewish. He once showed me his Russian passport where it was written that he was Jewish. Judaism in Russia is considered a nationality as well as a religion. They even have a region called Yevreska, the Jewish Autonomous Region in the Far East of Russia. Of the many regions of Russia, I never had an opportunity to visit Yevreska.

Where the Exodus tells us that Yahweh, the God of the Chosen People inspired and guided Moses to take the Jews out of Egypt, my mother believes that Moses was a leader with no influence from an inhuman entity. I do not know if her beliefs came out of her ethical humanism experiences or if something earlier in her life caused this. If you were to ask her if she were Jewish, she would emphatically say "Yes." If you followed up with "Does, she believes in God?" Her answer would be an equally emphatic "No."

For the longest time I agreed with her reasoning since I too felt the infinite connection to being a Jew but not being a member of the Jewish religion.

Where I was different from my mother is that I never considered myself a humanist, atheist, or agnostic. There was a God in my life. My earliest beliefs is that "God" was a higher being that was overly responsible for everything man was **not** able to explain. I felt a need to believe in God. It was God that helped me to deal with a series of troubling dreams (see My Dreams) I had and continued to have throughout my adolescents and youth. This belief never followed an organized religious belief. I did not believe in a Jewish God or a Christian God. I believed in my God, not the biblical scriptures. To simplify why I chose to believe in a "higher power" was because of a series of questions I asked myself,

"What came first, the chicken or the egg?" "If there is a beginning of everything, what was their before?" I wondered if I was a minimalist, philosopher or simply lost spiritually.

As I did not have scripture to guide me, I used meditation to communicate with my God. I remember spending time every day in meditation. Even if only for a few minutes at a time, the time I spent speaking to my God gave me some sense of relaxation I desperately needed. There were so many things I could not understand. It was obvious that no one in my family knew the answers to the questions I was asking so I turned to meditation. I certainly could not turn to my parents or siblings who were confessed atheists.

My siblings and I all entered marriages without knowing our ancestral lineage. I assume my siblings were equally unaware. My older brother may have known since he was closer to our

Grandfather William who may have shared his ancestry with him. Like my mother, I was never aware of my brother being a participant in anything having to do with religion and more importantly faith. I never remembered seeing anything Jewish in his home, not even a menorah. I have no memory of ever speaking with him about religion, faith, or even our cultural heritage.

When it finally came time to get married, I was the first of the kids. In my case, it happened soon after I turned 31 and the girl turned out to be a Levite Jew, and her brothers were descendants of Aaron as was I. I did not actually learn about this until our first meeting with the rabbi before our wedding. At 31, I still did not know about my Aaronides' heritage even then. (The marriage lasted 5 years.) It is important to admit to you here, that even though I learned of the Aaronides connection during our marriage it meant nothing to me at that time. In fact, we never discussed it. Her family was no more religious than mine. My younger sister married a Jewish man but not with the same ancestry.

According to tradition only your mother must be Jewish for a child to claim their Jewish ancestry but in the case of keeping the Levite bloodline intact, this is only passed on by the father. To keep track of this lineage is exceedingly difficult and therefore very precious.

3 Generations of American Levites

My parents were both born and raised in the Flatbush neighborhood in Brooklyn, NY in what was then an old New York Jewish neighborhood. Today it would be a miracle to find Jews living in the Flatbush neighborhood where they both grew up. My father was Bar Mitzvah'd, as was his father and every known generation of the Delugash and Cohen families. When my great grandfather came to the USA in the late 1880's he and his brothers came from Romania. When they entered the USA through Ellis Island in New York, the immigration official changed our family name from Delugash to Douglas. My Grandmother Carrie's (father's mother) line comes from what is now called Belarus (White Russia).

I am unaware if my mother was Bat-Mitzvah'd. She never mentioned it to me. I will assume she was not. My mother's family came from Lithuania and Ukraine.

Her Lithuanian ancestors emigrated to both the USA and South Africa. Their family names were Schneider and Groz (Gross). Her Ukrainian family were from Berdichev, Ukraine, a city outside the capital Kiev and known for Jewish citizenry. The Berdichev families were exceptionally large, and all murdered by Ukrainian Nazi sympathizers in Babi Yar, Ukraine in World War II. I had included photographs from the massacre but have since decided to delete them since they are so horrific. Each time I see photographs like these, I feel a pain as if part of me was with them.

My K-8 Education

My formal education started out in Chicago at a Jewish Day School called Anshe Emet. Anshe Emet was within walking distance of our 4-story apartment building at 2652 Lakeview Drive. There is now a high-rise condominium complex at this address. Due to my later acknowledged diagnosis of ADHD, I only lasted 4 years at Jewish Day School. I was unable to concentrate on my studies and unable to learn Hebrew which was a mandatory foreign language at the school. My inability to learn the modern language of Judaism has had various negative impacts on my life through the years. To this day I regret not having learned the language. I can speak words well once I have memorized them and I sing many of the songs I learned as a child.

A wonderful memory I would like to share was that my mother once told me that my "failure" to succeed at Anshe

Emet was not because I could not learn Hebrew, but rather because my teachers could not **teach me** Hebrew. My mother always had a way of making me feel better.

Anshe Emet Hebrew Day School

We had already moved to our new home while I was still at Anshe Emet. I finished my Jewish Day School experience after 4th grade. I was 10 years old. My parents arranged for me to stay in our new neighborhood for fifth grade at a public elementary school down the street from our new home. After spending a year at McCutcheon Elementary, my parents enrolled me in a well-known liberal arts school called Francis W Parker. The Parker School (FWP), a K-12 school, was located directly opposite the main entrance to Lincoln Park Zoo and had a large Jewish student population. It also had quite a few kids from well-to-do families from the North side of the city. I managed to stay at Parker until the end of 8th grade but that was all the school would allow. It was still 30 years before the first diagnosis of ADHD would be made in the USA. In hindsight it appears to have been a combination of ADHD and my inappropriate behaviors that contributed to my not lasting longer at Parker. I was friends with other kids that shared my dislike for the other kids in our classes. One owned a sailboat (a Rhodes 19) that we sailed on Lake Michigan at Montrose Harbor. One was the son of a well-known judge and the other the son of a successful architect who designed many of the hotels in Bangkok, Thailand in the 1960's and 1970's. I also spent time together with two brothers who taught me how to smoke. I remember it was April 14, 1973, and both brothers were removed from the school because their dad was gunned down in the driveway of their home by the Chicago Mafia. He was an enforcer for the Chicago mob and killed by his own people. I will let you do your own research here.

My 13th Year – Bar Mitzvah?

During the summer months between 7th and 8th grade, I traveled to Thailand with my father. During this trip we stopped in many countries including Japan, Hong Kong, Thailand, Vietnam, Cambodia, Laos, Iran, India, Italy, UK, and Israel. This trip gave me a great love of travel and a good start to achieving my travel to 105 countries.

Considering the US was still actively involved with the Viet Nam War, it was a summer filled with experiences that I can never forget. Aside from my experiences visiting Israel, the rest of my summer's experiences are unrelated to my journey other than it being part of my destiny.

My father found it necessary for me to come with him to Saigon, visit the Bridge on the River Kwai on the border of Cambodia and a quick visit to Vientiane, Laos during a Coup-de-Tat.

When my friends asked me how my summer was, I had endless stories to tell. Fortunately, I kept a journal of my trip which helped me tell the stories of which there were many. This journal became one of many that I would keep during my lifetime.

It was the summer of 1973. I had turned 13, the Jewish year for Bar' Mitzvah. I still did not know Hebrew and having been raised by ethical humanists, had not taken Bar' Mitzvah classes. My father accepted a UN/World Health Organization (WHO) appointment to teach at a dental school in Bangkok, Thailand for a two-month period. My siblings had other interests that summer, so my mother stayed home to take care of them, and my father and I set off on an "Around the World in 90 days" trip. On the way to Thailand, we stopped in Japan to visit my birthplace and then onto New Delhi, India. My father needed to meet with some people at WHO Headquarters in India.

We had an opportunity to take a side trip to see the Taj Mahal, which is one of the wonders of the world you never forget. I took a great photo of the Taj which is framed on a wall in my home. Certainly, the Mausoleum was an amazing palace like structure but for a 13-year-old, my strongest memory was seeing vultures on the side of the road eating the carcass of a dead water buffalo. I also saw a snake charmer outside the entrance to the Taj Mahal.

Taj Mahal, Agra, India

    The other memory I had was when my father and I were walking in Old Delhi, and we saw a water buffalo on top of a taxi. The driver was frantically trying to get the animal off his car but because buffalo were sacred in India he could only wait until the animal got off his vehicle. How he got on top of his car must have been an act of God.

Visit to Israel and my "True Jewish Awakening."

After leaving Bangkok, we had several stops prior to going to Israel. These stops were short but not insignificant and could well have played a subliminal role in my Jewish adventure. We spent a weekend in Saigon during the last presidential election in South Vietnam, a weekend in Tehran, Iran on the Shah's birthday and a stop in Laos during a coup-de-tat. If you ever meet me, ask me about these trips into the Arab world. Each stop had special memories. Although much later in life, I also minored in Islamic Studies at American University in the early 2000s. These studies gave me understanding of things I saw and witnessed in Tehran many years earlier.

1973 was an important year in American history and in hindsight still confuses me why my father took a trip into this part of the world at the time and with his 13-year-old son.

Saigon was still in the throes of the Vietnam War between South and North Vietnam. I have several vivid memories of my short weekend stay in Saigon. We stayed at the Park Hotel in downtown Saigon within walking distance of the clongs where military boats were parked, and near the main Post Office where I saw President Thieu drive up to place his vote in the election. At the time I had a small camera and unfortunately a big index finger that blocked the lens, so a photograph I took of him getting out of his limousine turned out to be a picture of my finger. Any chance of getting a picture in Time Magazine was gone.

When we came out of the hotel that morning, the first thing I saw was a one-legged Vietnamese shoeshine boy who said, "You number 1." Each street corner had Vietnamese military police with heavy weaponry behind piles of sandbags. My father let me walk around the back of the hotel where there was a public fountain. Several young

Vietnamese boys were in the fountain cooling off when two Vietnamese Military Police ran after then chasing them out of the fountain. I remember one of them raising his rifle in their direction and am so thankful they did not fire the weapon. That would have been a memory not to remember.

On that same trip my father and I had dinner with a Vietnamese Senator who lived on JFK Boulevard. She spoke with us about her feeling of how the USA got into the conflict in the beginning and how she wished it were different.

Our visit to Vientiane, Laos was very scary. In the morning, my father and I drove to the entrance of the Embassy of the Kuomintang. As he was adjusting his Rolo flex camera to take a picture down the driveway toward the main gate, a soldier was raising a missile launcher on his shoulder pointed in our direction. I was able to convince my father to stop taking the picture so we could return to the taxi. After we returned to our hotel we went to the rooftop where a reporter for the Chicago Sun Times was calling in a report that two Laotian generals were strafing the streets with machine guns attached to biplanes they took off from in Bangkok. They were attempting a coup of the government but failed. What is most bizarre is that they took off and returned to a landing strip near the University where my father was teaching; and were executed by a firing squad outside the Dental School where he taught. My father would never discuss this with me.

Our visit to Tehran was more about purchasing souvenirs, or so I thought. It happened to be the birthday of Sha Pahlavi. My dad left me in the hotel to take a private meeting at the Presidential Palace. In the afternoon we took a walk in the downtown area of Tehran. We went into a café that sold pita bread. I particularly remember being stared at by the men in the café.

Israel

We eventually visited Tel Aviv in Israel. It was holiday time, and most places were closed in the capital. We went to visit Old Jerusalem to visit the Holocaust Museum and the Wailing Wall.

I will never forget what I saw there that day. Exhibits of eyewear and piles of shoes were in cases with explanations of where they were from with photographs of Auschwitz Jews in their Nazi prison uniforms.

I saw the eyes of the Jews in the photographs. I felt their eyes burning into my soul. Stares of confusion, no understanding of what was happening to them, why it was happening or what their ultimate destinies were. 50 years have passed and the visions I saw at the Holocaust Museum in Old Jerusalem remain a permanent sketch in my memory. What I saw that day triggered a nerve that incensed me to be overly aware of my being a Jew. I am sure, without doubt, that my emotional state was forever changed after that day. When the film "Schindler's List" was released in 1993, twenty years later, it revitalized all the feelings I had in Old Jerusalem.

Our visit to the Wailing Wall was an entirely different type of experience. I had seen photographs of the Wall when I did research before our trip. It was exciting to see the real thing but outside of "Fiddler on the Roof," I knew so little of Jewish history to understand and fully appreciate what I was experiencing. At the foot of the Wall were dozens of rabbi's praying. They were praying alone. There was no one individual leading the prayers. Each rabbi was in his own time and space. Most of them had long beards and appeared to be Hassidic Jews. As the Wall is thousands of years old it has many holes in its façade.

There were rolled paper notes stuffed in many of the holes. I assume these were prayer notes.

As we stood there one of the Jewish Rabbi's approached us offering to conduct a Bar Mitzvah. How many Jewish 13-year-old boys are given the ultimate opportunity to have their Bar Mitzvah at *the* Wailing Wall, the only remains of the Temple of David?

Typical of my father, he looked at his watch and said that if I wanted to do the Bar Mitzvah, I would not have time to get a camel ride. I do not think we had even discussed the possibility of a camel ride up to that point. I opted for the camel ride. I do not think this was a sign that I would be saved in 2007, but it certainly stresses my point that God and religion had no significance to my parents.

Before returning to Chicago, my father and I also visited Rome and London. I came home alone as my father decided to stay in England to plan for his soon-to-be new wife to travel with him. They met during our trip.

Soon after returning to Chicago, and the eventual return of my father, my parents officially separated. I stayed with my mother. My siblings moved in with my father. We were all in the same neighborhood in Chicago but considering how dysfunctional our family had become, we could have been in completely different cities. My parents soon divorced.

The High School Years.
My Coming of Age.

I spent the first half of my first year of high school at a north side Chicago public high school called Senn High. Nicholas Senn High was one of those public mega high schools with 5,000 students. Class sizes were so large that teachers never took attendance since they would have had no time to teach the lessons if they spent time calling out the names of the students. In other words, no one ever knew if I was there or not. Except for the first day of school, I did not return to classes.

Nichoas Senn High School

On the first day of school, I met a bunch of kids who I regrettably got mixed up with. As much as I may have pretended to be the strong middle child, the recent divorce of my parents and division of the family was extremely hard on me. I certainly did not understand this at the time but considering what happened next is evident of many deep-rooted emotional issues I was not dealing with. Soon after meeting these kids, I was spending time together with them every day instead of going to school. I think the school may have sent one note home to my parents but that was about all they cared. We all spent time together at the neighborhood Jack in the Box and a nearby car wash. I remember becoming friendly with the men who worked at the car wash. I may have only been 14 going on 15 but I was already 6' tall and it was just a year after my summer trip of 1973.

Saved by an Angel?

I was at the home of one of the kids, not too far from the High School. He had a substance he said was hash, but it was laced with something stronger. I had smoked marijuana once or twice during my summer camp years, so I went along with the group and smoked the substance. Whatever I did smoke that afternoon took its toll on my brain. I was without question "stoned." When I left the apartment, I was not able to walk very well and went to the back alley of the car wash between the apartment and the school. It was early December, and the ground was covered with snow. I was wearing a long Army style coat which served as both a ground cover and a blanket. I lay down on the snow in the alley and fell fast asleep. I have no idea how long I was asleep, but I woke up to the sound of someone saying, "Is he dead?"

As I looked up there were 3 of the car wash attendants staring down at me. I seem to recall I knew them from hanging around the car wash in previous days (playing hooky). I told them I was fine, which obviously was not the case.

I do not know what happened next, but my memory is that I was standing at the front door of my house. I have no memory between getting up from the snow to showing up at my front door. Someone, my personal angel, took me from the car wash to my house. It was a good 2 miles between the school and my house. When I rang the doorbell (I do not know why I did not use my keys) my mother answered the door. She took me upstairs to my bedroom and put me in bed. I was very cold, and she put several blankets on top of me. I fell into a deep sleep.

When I woke up it was early evening. I realized that I was late for a date with my then girlfriend. I tried to pull myself together. When I went downstairs my mother was in the kitchen and asked me why I was getting dressed. I reminded her that I had a date. She told me that she had already called the girl's parents to say I would not be there. She also told me that two days had passed. I was asleep for more than 60 hours.

As this was December and at the end of my Fall term, my parents took me out of Senn High and arranged for me to transfer to St. John's Military Academy, a dormitory college prep school located in Delafield, Wisconsin, far from Senn High and far from my life in Chicago. The idea of a military school stemmed from an interest I had developed when I was still at Parker. I joined a book club and ordered quite a few books on the history of World War II.

Time to straighten up!

St. John's was an enormous shock in every sense. I was a 14-year-old kid totally mixed up and misguided from a recently divorced and highly dysfunctional family entering a completely structured life run by kids not more than 4 years my senior. St. John's was like college military academies in that new students/cadets were called plebes, or "new boys."

We were required to stand at attention against the wall of the hallway every time an "old boy" passed us. Each morning we would be required to stay in our rooms after waking up and getting dressed. When the bugle call came for breakfast, we would have to stand outside our dorm room doors standing at attention. On Saturday mornings we had room inspections, and they would tear my room apart every time. There was some level of sense to the whole thing. We all believed it was just a way for all the cadets to get back at their sergeants by doing to the new cadets what was done to them. More of the "eye for an eye." When we stood at attention, we were required to stick our shoulders back and scrunch our chins to our chest and yell "Yes, sir!" whenever spoken to. Whenever we would fail in our duties, which in my case happened every few minutes we were told to "drop and give me twenty" which referred to dropping to the floor and doing twenty pushups.

The very first week I was at St. John's, one of the soon to be graduating seniors came into my room and while I was asleep applied Prell Concentrate to my toes and lit it on fire, a.k.a. a "hot foot." I awoke with a start and saw no one there but it was enough of a fright that I took my own clothes (civi's) out of my trunk (we wore school uniforms) and ran away from school. I called my parents from a phone outside of town. My father then called the Admissions Director who accepted me to the school. He was also the golf coach. My father told me to wait at a certain place and he would drive up from Chicago. What I did not expect was the Admissions counselor to show up instead. He took me back to his house which was located on the campus golf course. He convinced me to stay.

After a short investigation of the incident, the senior admitted what he did and was expelled from the school. I was never "hazed" again after that first week but went through a complete intensive "new boy" training for a good 12 weeks.

Being a cadet in "D" Delta Company was a wonderful experience and I soon started to become a better person, more responsible and respectable. As much as I may have hated to be there at times when I look back on my St. John's experiences they are forever remembered as the best part of my childhood.

Main Drag of Delta Company

Soon after my first month at St. John's I auditioned for and became a member of the Episcopalian all boys church choir. I should note that for the 5 summers prior to the summer of '73, my parents sent me to a theatre performance camp called Harand Camp, in Elkhart Lake, Wisconsin since I loved to sing. I had wonderful, wonderful memories from Harand and as I mentioned earlier, would love to share if we ever meet.

Harand Camp, Elkhart Lake, Wisconsin

St. John's had its own Victory Memorial Chapel. Church services that were held twice a week. The choir head and my science teacher was Mr. Robert Ausland, a robust man, who sadly went to our maker soon after I graduated. He took a personal interest in me and became an emotional guide in my development at St. John's.

He was also responsible for archery, which was in the basement of the Chapel and head of the drama club which I of course was continually active in.

Aside from Mr. Ausland, another person at St. John's that played a key role in my development and my becoming a young man was Sergeant Major William Golden. "Smadge" as we referred to him, was my "father" and mentor for the next 3 years of my life.

SGM Golden

A caricature done of the two of us by a peer.

My first introduction to the *"God of the Christians"* and Scripture...

During my time with the church choir, I became one of two soloists. It was a requirement that all students at St. John's write down their religious affiliation on their applications. I admitted I was Jewish even though there were very few known Jewish kids attending the school. Most of the other Jewish kids were members of Band Company. We sang at many events outside of the school including a concert at a mausoleum in Milwaukee once. I deliberately did not verbalize the name Jesus or Christ when it was part of a choir hymn. For some reason I believed that because I was "Jewish" to verbalize His name was against my own religion.

While at St. John's the President of the school, Edison B Lerch a WWI retired Major, believed that all cadets should kneel during prayer services. I refused on account of my Jewish religion. I did not have a clue that kneeling was even mentioned in the Old Testament. As I look back on this period in my life it seems ridiculous since I was hardly raised a Jew, but I knew enough about Judaism and used my inherited religion as an excuse not to accept Major Lerch's rules. I had more than one meeting in his office and after each discussion with him he continued to insist that I follow School rules at Chapel. At one point he gave me an alternative, saying that I could stand and extend my arms to the sky which is what he told me proper Jews do in temple worship. Being the argumentative independent middle-child, I had become in my childhood I called my retired politician father who made a visit to the school. who convinced Maj. Lerch that I could sit during these periods.

My First Baptism

My math teacher, and dormitory resident-teacher Mr. Orloff, attended a Baptist Congregation in neighboring Pewaukee, Wisconsin. He encouraged me and some of his other students to go off campus to his church. Giving me an opportunity to get away from the military life once per week, I accepted his invitation. During one of these visits, I was invited to be baptized and agreed to be baptized by repeating words recited to me by the Minister. There was no holy water used for the baptism. I do not know if I took it all seriously or was putting on an act considering everything else that was happening at school with the choir, especially with my refusal to verbally speak the name of our Lord and refusal to kneel in services.

It was just another ruse I used to take advantage of the system. It was another way for me to get time off-campus and away from the military life.

We were also allowed to wear our civi's (non-military clothes) which for some reason always seemed to me another benefit worth the commitment to attend the Church services. One positive note that did come out of my visits to the Church group is that it started me on reading scripture.

When I was finishing high school and was searching for universities to attend, I made an appointment to interview at the Hebrew Union College in New York City. Even though I was not by any means religious, I felt like I had a calling to do something great and thought that I should study to be a Cantor. My mother came with me to New York. The interview was one of the most embarrassing interviews I have ever had. The admissions counselor asked me why they should accept me since I did not have a Bar' Mitzvah nor could I read Hebrew. I tried to convince him that I loved to sing but I did not convince him. I took this denial badly.

If there was any "religious" Judaism in me, it left me that day. This was the first time I had taken a step to join the Jewish religious community and was turned away. In retrospect I was kidding myself traveling to New York to get into HUC with no religious Jewish credentials.

The last thing I did before ending my two years stay at Chicago's Columbia College School of Theatre and Communications was direct a 1 act play called "Answers" by Tom Topor. The play was about a man who was arrested with a count of murder. Two police officers interrogated what we presume was an honest man and convinced him he was guilty using tactics including the term "which came first? The chicken or the egg?" This was not too far off my own question that kept me within reach of God but not yet a believer.

1980's – My Twenties
College and The University Years –
The Lone Jew of Catholic U becomes the *Defender of the Jews.*

My stepfather transferred his job from Chicago to Gaithersburg, Maryland in the fall of 1979 and we moved to Gaithersburg at Christmas. Once we moved to Maryland, I transferred to a local University, The Catholic University of America. I chose this school because they had a well-known School of Drama called the Hartke School of Drama. When I finished my 2nd year at Colombia, I managed to leave with a perfect 4.0 grade point average. The admissions counselor at Catholic did not look very carefully at my transcripts and assumed I was a 4.0 student at Columbia University in New York, not Columbia College in Chicago.

Soon after we moved to Gaithersburg, my grandmother Rose died. She had been living in an assisted living home in Evanston, Illinois for several years after suffering a major stroke. She had little recollection of who she was at the end of her life. She was my favorite grandparent. I named my daughter after her. She meant a lot to me though my entire life. I do not have any sense that she participated in my life in a spiritual sense, but I think of her often and hope I will be able to see her again one day.

For no particularly known reason I was the only undergraduate registered Jewish student at Catholic University. Unlike St. John's, it was not required to tell the University your religious affiliation. I knew of other Jewish students, but they all chose to be anonymous in their registrations. Most of them attended the Kennedy School of Law. In my second year at Catholic University, I became the President of the Jewish Student Organization (JSO).

The outgoing President had decided to transfer to American University since it had a large and very public Jewish community. He passed the reins on to me. I do not seem to recall there were any other registered Jews available to take over.

Although I was the only officially registered Jew in the organization it was the largest student organization at Catholic University with more than 75 members. The rest were a combination of Irish and Roman Catholics. Their reason for being members of the Organization was so they could attend the annual Passover Seder, which was well known on campus. The University food service had a rule that for any University club wishing to use the cafeteria food service as a caterer all participants had to be members of the organization.

During my time as the President of the JSO at Catholic, I brought several high-profile Jewish speakers to the campus including the acclaimed and prolific writer Chaim Potok and the son of Moshe Dayan.

Chaim Potok

My guest speaker's visits to the University came with protests from a large group of Palestinian students who attended Catholic University. Ironic is that I was very sociable with this group. I made it a habit to hang out at the coffee shop at the University which was also frequented by members of the International House where the Palestinian students lived. We shared many political conversations together but never discussed Judaism, Christianity, or the Muslim religion This is a good thing since at the time I knew extraordinarily little of my own religion and faith. I do not recall that any of us were knowledgeable in Torah or the Koran. An outsider might assume that because they were attending the Catholic University that had Christian beliefs versus Muslim which could also explain why we did not have religious confrontations. I do not know what their beliefs were.

Because they knew I was Jewish, something hard to ignore since I was the President of the JSO, I became their target for everything about Israel and the PLO. They eventually nicknamed me "The Lone Jew of Catholic U." They decided that since I was Catholic University's resident Jew, I was responsible for defending Israel in all our discussions and Coffee House debates.

Since I knew extraordinarily little of what was really happening, I decided to bring first the son of Moshe Dayan and then Chaim Potok to speak at the University. I particularly remember that when Dayan came to the University, they flew the unofficial flag of the PLO in front of the International House. The FBI came to the House and removed it. When Chaim Potok came to the University to speak, they all came to the event ready to argue with him. Not one word came out of any of their mouths. They, like the rest of us, were awestruck at his words and could only listen to his speech. There were not even any questions afterwards.

Chaim Potok exhibited enormous personal strength in his speech and the effect it had on his listening audience, especially the young Palestinians had, like many things in my life, an effect and impression which changed us all. After his speech I was once again revitalized as the *Defender of the Jews*.

Not Judaism, not Israel, but the Jews themselves. Now that I was in my 20's I started to become aggressive in my response to others who challenged me as a Jew. My memories of visiting the Holocaust Museum 8 years earlier were still extraordinarily strong as well, which enforced my ability to believe this way. Having found a new interest in being a Jew, I decided to add theology as a minor in my junior year. Unlike others who took theology to better understand Catholicism or other religions, I took it purposely to best understand what I believed were the weaknesses of global religions, information that would aid me in arguments I might have with religious people. My studies included Catholicism, Christianity, Judaism, Islam, and other Eastern and Asian religions. It made me read enormous amounts of scripture.

Following the completion of my Junior Year at Catholic University I met a girl doing summer-stock theatre at Montgomery College in Rockville, MD.

She attended Towson State University near Baltimore. Like my earlier experience going to a small Baptist Church with my math teacher, one of her professors convinced her to go with him to visit a small off-campus Presbyterian congregation. To emphasize that my ideology of defending the Jews was not a religious ideology, the girl was a Presbyterian. For most of the summer, aside from admitting to each other what our familial religions were, we never spoke of religion. Since we were both "theatre people" that was the center of our conversations versus religion and politics.

I used to travel from my home in Gaithersburg, Maryland to Towson every other weekend to visit her. Before one weekend she told me on the phone that she started attending services with a small Presbyterian Church near her dorm. She told me about her newfound religious beliefs. This I felt would destroy our relationship. I had no interest in dating a born-again Christian. In her case it was not the spirit that got hold of her but rather the professor who was taking her there. I told her I wanted to go with her to the service that weekend which I did.

I considered this another opportunity to battle the enemy. With my newfound theological education from Catholic University, during one of our conversations on scripture she quoted versus from both the Old and New Testament, where the Old Testament would ask the question and the New Testament verse offered the answer. In fact, she had these little snips of paper the size of a fortune cookie message. One of the things we were taught while attending Sunday school at the Chicago Ethical Humanist society was that the Bible was a book of stories and to be careful of Christians quoting scripture with single verses. When I read scripture, I read the chapters from start to finish before attempting to analyze their meaning. When I read what she had been quoted by her minister I argued that he was falsely interpreting scripture to prove his claims. I convinced her that I knew this since I was studying for a Minor in Theology at Catholic University.

Being the *Defender of the Jews* I decided to become a Defender of Scripture (according at least to my interpretation). I attended the service with her and confronted the Minister after the service. The Minister asked me if I was saved. When I told him that I was baptized earlier he then asked me if I was a believer and if I had faith. I could not answer that and proceeded to make my argument that his interpretation of the verses did not match well with the overall scripture he was quoting from and there was much he was not telling his congregants. His answer was that his congregants could only understand so much which is why he rarely discussed entire chapters. I do not think I had even checked to see if his quotes were interpreted correctly or not. I just needed an excuse to argue with him and hope I could stop my girlfriend from attending services. She stopped at my request.

1983 – 1990: The Silent Years.

After her graduation in 1983, I followed her to New Haven, CT where we both worked in different regional theatres exploring our theatrical careers and dreams. Eventually we went our separate ways. I moved from New Haven to Philadelphia and then back to the Washington DC area. We did not separate due to religion. I took a job with an international company and spent the rest of the decade traveling all over the world. I have no memory of attending temple, church or reading scripture during that time.

This period of my life was from a business perspective my years of maturing as a businessman and traveling to over 100 countries. Unless I purposely forgot, I don't know why God was not a memorable part of this time.

The 1990s. My Thirties

Since the 80s were just a blur in my 40-year journey, onwards to my thirties and the 90's.

I was not aware of my ancestry as a descendant of the Aaronides (Levites) (Numbers 18. 1–7)[1] until my early thirties. One might think that an ancestral relationship as important as mine would be discussed in my upbringing but in my case, I was not raised in a typical Jewish household, nor was my family a member of a local temple or synagogue.

There would be a time in my early thirties when my mother and I attended high holy day services at a synagogue in Silver Spring, Maryland. During the service, the first reading of Torah, called the Aleyah, was given on behalf of the congregation. To read the Aleyah, you had to be a Cohen Jew. (Cohen, also

---

[1] See end of book for this scripture.

called Levites, were Aaronides Jews). The prayers were completely in Hebrew, a language I did not know. I had a chance to learn it when I attended elementary Jewish day school but that did not come to fruition. I do remember that the rabbi at the synagogue was not allowed to be in the prayer circle as he was not a Cohen, Levite, or a living descendent of Aaron.

In 1991, I married a Jewish girl whose parents were both Levites. This was completely unintentional since a mutual theatre friend introduced us who was not Jewish and had no idea or awareness of the bloodline. Several years after we were married, I determined it was necessary for me to move to Russia which I did in August 1994. She was to follow a month later but did not arrive until 9 months later. Living in Russia did not appeal to her and within the 2nd week of her trip she decided to return home early and without warning she filed for divorce.

The True Beginning of my Journey to Christ

Two years after I moved to Russia, and just months after my divorce was official, I met my current wife. She was working for another company in the same building where I had my office. The building was an Institute located in St. Petersburg (Leningrad), Russia.

She was everything of which I had ever dreamed. Funny thing is that I made a promise to myself that I would take my time before considering another marriage. God obviously had other ideas for me. We were married less than 10 months from the day we met. For diplomatic reasons we had to get married outside of Russia. At the time, the USA was not an option, so we were married in a small ceremony in a Russian restaurant in Helsinki, Finland. The marriage was conducted by a civil magistrate who spoke English and some Russian. I had many special friends in

Helsinki, so I was able to arrange a best man and matron of honor. It was a nice quaint event with a wonderful banquet. My bride, who is now my wife and mother of my wonderful children, was gorgeous.

We remained in Russia for another 3 years and came to the US in mid-July of 2000 when she was 7 months pregnant with our first child.

Back in the USA

When we returned to the US we moved in with my mother and stepfather to their townhouse in Silver Spring, Maryland. We stayed there until after our son was born. We rented an apartment in Gaithersburg for the next first few years as I adjusted to being an American again. We lived in Gaithersburg near to where I lived when I first moved to Gaithersburg from Chicago in 1979. As the neighborhood started to get worse with crime and constant police sirens, we took advantage of the low mortgage market and bought a new home in the Eastern Panhandle of West Virginia.

During the last 2 of 3 years that we lived in Gaithersburg, I enrolled in the graduate program at American University (AU). When we first returned to the USA, it was exceedingly difficult to find work without a master's degree. I finally found a job but decided I should still get a master's degree in case I should become unemployed and needed this on my resume. I became a student at the School of International Studies at AU. AU SIS was heavily attended by students from the Middle East. As an invasion of Iraq became imminent many of the students from the region started to leave Washington and return home. A number of these students were members of Royal families in Qatar and elsewhere. While at AU I also took two classes in Islamic Studies. I was very curious to know more about Islam considering what was happening on the world stage after September 11th, 2001.

I have fond memories of my History of Islam course. I was not the only Jewish student in the class. In fact, the other known Jewish student was the head of a major Free Palestine organization. Some of the American students (women) were Muslims and chose to wear the hijab over their heads. I was very vocal in the class. Admittedly I was incredibly surprised in what I learned about who Mohammed was, his military background as a General of his Army and his many Jewish concubines he took after killing their husbands in acts of war.

I was appalled that an entire religious community, now considered the largest single religion in the world could have a prophet who murdered so many before becoming a prophet of God. When I would ask questions, it upset the Muslim students.

At one point the teacher asked for a private meeting where he asked me if I had other reasons for attending the course and asking so many poignant questions. I assured him that I had no previous issues with Islam or Muslims and that my questions were geared to better understand the books we were reading. He accepted my explanation and asked me to continue with my questions as it made his class livelier. He shared with me that he usually had little discussion in his class which he attributed to the shock many of his Muslim students had when reading about what the prophet of their religion did before becoming the prophet.

West Virginia and IBC

Teaching The Bible As It Is For People As They Are.

Soon after moving into our new home in West Virginia, we met a family who we remain in touch with today. They attended a church called the Independent Bible Church (IBC) in Martinsburg, WV. The mother of the brood told my wife that there was a Ukrainian woman who attended IBC. My wife soon became friends with this woman, who like her was married to an American. The Ukrainian American woman had moved to the USA many years earlier with her family. They left the Ukraine as Jewish refugees. She however accepted Christ after marrying her American husband. With the encouragement of both families, we started attending regular Sunday services at IBC in early 2006. My oldest child was 5-years old.

The IBC experience was the first continuous religious activity I had other than attending Chapel services at St. John's in high school. It was my first adult experience. It was also the beginning of my adult transformation which would result in my awakening and enlightenment to becoming a "Saved Jew." The first time we attended a Sunday service, I heard the voices of the small but blessed choir, and I knew that I wanted to join the choir, but this was completely impossible since I was not a believer in their God.

The IBC Praise Team

In fact, I was still very much opposed to "religion" as I had been for years. I became amazingly comfortable attending IBC services and even attending some of their prayer meetings and adult bible classes but made it clear to the pastors of the church that I was a non-believer. I felt less threatened telling them this up front so that they would leave me alone in a sense.

Through the approximately 1 year that led up to my "Surrender to God", there were several events that, in retrospect, I feel had a profound impact on me.

On any given Sunday we would not be aware of the topic of the sermon in advance yet mysteriously it would touch on a sensitive subject that was the source of a marital disagreement the day before.

Pastor Mark

The lead pastor at the Church, Mark Johnson, did this on many occasions.

In the fall of 2006, I decided to take a class at the Church taught by their Pastor George Michael, who amongst other things taught the Old Testament.

Pastor George

It was based on the Proverbs and Psalms of the Old Testament. Since the Old Testament was the Jewish Bible, I convinced myself that it was OK to study it. Even though I had read the New Testament when studying theology at Catholic University years before, I was still uncomfortable reading and interpreting the New Testament since I did not accept Jesus as the Savior of the Jewish people. By this time, I did acknowledge his existence as a Jewish rabbi but not as far as the Christians believed. I remember telling Pastor George that I was not a believer.

After my experiences with the Presbyterian minister in Towson, MD I had created my own little war and was destined to prove that the claims of the New Testament were all false. When I would discuss this with my wife, she would remind me that belief is based on "Faith." No matter how many times she told me this I refused to accept it.

During the Old Testament class, one of the students made a comment I found offensive. On the way to work the next morning, I stopped at the bookstore at Washington DC's Union Station and bought a book called "To be a Jew." I read the book and decided that after 50 years, I wanted to learn how to be a Jew. After all my failed attempts, my experiences at IBC encouraged me to become more familiar with Judaism and tradition.

Since I was still in my own private war with the God of the Christians, I decided that I should find a Jewish

Temple or Synagogue. I stopped going to classes and stopped attending Sunday services at IBC. I no longer considered myself a wandering Jew and decided I was going to become a Born-Again Jew. (Fortunately, this was short-lived) I became extremely interested in finding a Synagogue in nearby Hagerstown, Maryland but this did not materialize.

    I related this to something I would call "Prerequisites to God's Chosen People." Part of my negative attitude toward organized religion stemmed from the Ethical Humanist Society and the refusal by Hebrew Union College to allow me to enroll in their Cantor School because I had not been Bar Mitzvah'd and did not know Hebrew. It certainly made sense, but I still reacted to it in this way. The Hagerstown Synagogue said that you must first join them before you can attend their services. I later learned that this was not exactly true, and although they preferred attendees to be members it was not a requirement.

So, if I wanted to be a Jew why did all of this bother me? It was a problem because in truth I had no idea of what I really wanted. I was at war with Jesus Christ, I was at war with Judaism, and I was carrying angry memories from my childhood that I did not come to terms with. I was in dire need of a spiritual guide. I did not know how to reach out, but I started meditating again and asking the God I knew to help me find my way.

After a little over a month of not going to IBC I made the decision that we should return. If I could not believe as members of the IBC community believed at least I knew they would be good to my family, and I really did not want to ruin any relationships we had established during the previous year. When we returned, we established a regular seating area on the balcony of the sanctuary. The sanctuary itself is small enough that even in the balcony the view is still particularly good and close enough that you do not have to squint to see the Pastor or the screen where they show the words for the Sunday songs.

I purposely kept my distance from the Church's Teacher-Pastor, Pastor Mark. I had profound respect for him but every Sunday he closed his sermons inviting non-believers to accept the Lord and to join him at the front of the sanctuary. He would ask this question during his closing prayer so our eyes would be closed. As a non-believer I would watch to see if anyone would raise their hand or walk to the front of the congregation. I do not remember anyone ever walking to the front but did see occasional hands go up. What I thought I saw on more than one occasion was Pastor Mark looking up in my direction. I felt like he was reaching out to me every time he made this invitation. I wanted to be sure that if the day ever came, that I made the decision to go to him, that it would be a long walk to get there. I wanted to be sure I had an opportunity to go out the exit door when I got to the main floor instead of continuing to the front of the congregation.

The Sanctuary   The Balcony

There were times I was ready to take the walk to the front. On each occasion as I would attempt to stand up, my feet would fall asleep and then my legs. Every time I wanted to take the walk this happened. I have heard that the Devil acts in mysterious ways in his constant battle to keep people from becoming believers. I truly believe this is what was happening to me, not only on the balcony of the sanctuary at IBC but throughout my life every time I came close to God.

Secretly, I wanted so much to believe. Secretly, I was so jealous that I was not a part of this wonderful community of believers. Never had I experienced the comfort of belonging. Even though I had not accepted "their" God I was still accepted as one of them. This stirred jealousy in me and created a sense of loss and separation from the group since I was not able to feel what they felt. I wanted the Lord to enter my soul and take away the burden I had lived with most of my life.

Saturday, January 7th, 2007
The Day of my Spiritual *Awakening*

What exactly happened? I did not wake up that morning and make a profound faith-based decision to accept Jesus as my Savior. When I went to sleep the night before I was still happy being the cordial, but obnoxious, aggressive debater of faith-based religious beliefs. Something happened between the time I went to sleep and the time I awoke the next morning that would change my life forever. The Father made His decision that it was my time and sent the Spirit to enter my soul and opened my eyes to our Savior Jesus Christ. I am now a Saved Jew, a completed Jew, a Messianic Jew, a devout member of His Chosen People. I am now His.

Did I experience an Epiphany?

I think I did. And I also believe it has had everlasting effects on my life. According to the Oxford dictionary an epiphany is "a moment of sudden revelation or insight."

There have been many occasions over the last 17+ years that I have trusted God and things have worked out. Some of these things have been job related, others personal or family. I do not suggest that my problems were solved but that they could have been far more serious than they had become.

I have faith in God that cannot waver. The one thing that never changes in my life is that I am one with Him. I certainly have my ups and downs but at the end of the day, it either works out or I simply come to the realization that I never needed it any other way to start.

For a long time, my wife and I had situations when something was happening in our lives, and we did not know how to answer certain questions. I was not a believer during these times, so faith was not an option. On a Saturday, we would have a serious discussion on a topic in our lives and the next day, as we were listening to Pastor Mark give his sermon at IBC, he would include the answer to our questions. *Every time*. It was uncanny. How was this even possible? **Faith. Faith. Faith**.

I continue to have these experience every time I hear Pastor Mark's sermons.

Baptism

Soon after I accepted Jesus Christ as my Savior, I decided I wanted to join the Independent Bible Church and be an official member. The Church's bylaws only accept believers who have publicly testified their Faith through public Baptism. I applied for membership just one week after I accepted our Savior. Pastor Mark Johnson, the Pastor-Teacher (that I spent so much effort staying away from) told me that one of the rules of the Independent Bible Church (IBC) is that all members must first be Baptized by immersion. This is something I had not done when I was 16. He explained that sprinkling of water is not accepted by IBC as a true baptism. IBC feels the immersion represents Christ's death and rebirth. It is also important to remember that my experience at 16 was not honest.

On April 22nd, 2007, I participated in the Church's Baptismal Sunday and went through official immersion and was baptized. The choir's anthem that day was "Step into the Water." They had sung this several weeks earlier but decided to sing it that morning just for me since I had also joined the choir after becoming a member.

Prayer – The True Foundation of Faith

When I woke up that joyous Sunday morning and accepted the Spirit into my soul. I felt so exuberant that I wanted to tell everyone I knew. I never did this as the lone Jew of Catholic U. When I spoke to my IBC friends, now my new brothers and sisters in Christ, they told me they had been praying ever since meeting me, that one day I would accept our Savior. They were so happy to hear of the news. They said that the angels in Heaven must be having the biggest party ever celebrating my awakening. Pastors Mark, Curt Lowry, Choir leader Brent Alderman (now with the Lord), George, and other Pastoral staff at the Church also told me they had been praying for me.

At IBC, nothing is more important than prayer. Some years ago, I participated with my wife in an Adult Bible Fellowship class, called "Disciples," we spent more than half of the class time in prayer.

Each participant in the group offered testimony about themselves, family members and people they knew who were having difficulties and needed prayer. Everyone printed the names which they would all pray for during the week until the next time we would meet. Midway through the class someone would offer up a prayer asking the Lord to bless all the people just mentioned. In addition to requests for prayers we occasionally offered, raises for things the Lord had done during the past week. Regrettably, we did not offer enough praise, but asking for prayer seems to be very common in the church and perhaps across the world.

In my first year as a child of our Savior I wanted to see if I could find a Messianic Jewish Temple where I could be a saved Jew. At IBC I was the only Jewish member. I brought my family to a

Messianic Temple in Columbia, Maryland. Their style of prayer was quite different.

As in Jewish temples I attended in the past, everything but the sermon by the rabbi, included reading scripture from the Bible and prayer books. Everyone read the same Hebrew or English verses together. No one spoke from the heart using their own words. Only God's inspired words were spoken during the Sabbath service. In this service, the Sabbath was remarkably like what Jesus would have done in temple during his lifetime on Earth. The rabbi then offered a sermon about Jesus which confirmed the Messianic part of their Sabbath service.

When my mother and I attended the Yom Kippur services in the early 90's, at Temple Shalom in Silver Spring, Maryland, the Aaronides-Levite members of the congregation were asked to the front of the congregation to give the

Aliyah, to pray to God on behalf of everyone else. It was that day I learned I was a descendant of the High Priest of the Israelites.

Even the rabbi was not able to pray in that setting as he was not Aaronides. Although awkward since I could not speak Hebrew, I still became part of the prayer circle and watched those around me who in some ways were all related.

17 Years Later

It has now been 17 years since that blessed day. There have been troubled times but through all these experiences, I have never lost sight of who I was and no matter how difficult life became, I have had **faith** that everything would work out. And it has.

IBC has continued to play a major role in my staying the course. Over these many years, IBC has greatly expanded their pastoral staff and programs. There are two services each Sunday morning with loads of ABFs available to attend if you come for the entire morning. One special Adult Bible Fellowship is held during the second service in the Fellowship Hall which is located underneath the sanctuary. I have held two Messianic Passover Seders in this room in past years.

Pastor Curt

The teacher-pastor who leads this particular ABF is also the lead pastor for senior programs, Pastor Curt Lowry. Over these nearly twenty years of attending IBC, he and his wife Robyn (now with the Lord), became very good friends of the family. I continue to attend his classes when I can out of my great respect for Pastor Curt. The classes are always full.

The subject matter he picks is always lively and always scriptural. When he is teaching Old Testament scripture I like to get into these discussion as a completed Jew. I have a feeling of responsibility to my Jewish faith that they be fairly represented in these discussions. Not sure why I continue to feel this way.

Children's Ministries at IBC

When we first started coming to IBC Children's Ministries was very different. It has grown tremendously through the years and now has a strong AWANA program on Wednesday's, a large Kids program where my youngest still attends and a Kid's Music Ministry, led by Pastor of Music, **Dave Marion**. In the old days, Children's Ministries was run by **Pastor Randy Bradley** (see my Focus on him later in the book) and is now led by **Pastor Chris Marion** who does an incredible job mentoring to a staff working with hundreds of kids every week.

A Special Thank You!

I have said a lot about the Independent Bible Church, its pastoral staff and their impact on my coming to the Lord. The one group I did not include in my original manuscript but are so important to my Journey are the families that have befriended us over the years. There are a group of rather large families (and some a bit smaller); A group of very special people, all of which are my brothers and sisters in Christ. They are all in some way or another, related to IBC. Many are still members or come to IBC either for sermons, ABFs, choir, AWANA or other events. Some have gone on to new churches born from IBC. Some have moved away from the area. But no matter where they are today, I wanted to thank all of them for being such an important and loving part of my continued Journey over the last 20 years.

- Steven

Supplements

Scriptural reference – What is an Aaronides Jew?

Duties of Priests and Levites

> **18** The Lord said to Aaron, "You, your sons and your family are to bear the responsibility for offenses connected with the sanctuary, and you and your sons alone are to bear the responsibility for offenses connected with the priesthood. ² Bring your fellow Levites from your ancestral tribe to join you and assist you when you and your sons minister before the tent of the covenant law. ³ They are to be responsible to you and are to perform all the duties of the tent, but they must not go near the furnishings of the sanctuary or the altar. Otherwise, both they and you will die. ⁴ They are to join you and be responsible for the care of the tent of meeting—all the work at the tent—and no one else may come near where you are.

⁵ "You are to be responsible for the care of the sanctuary and the altar, so that my wrath will not fall on the Israelites again. ⁶ I myself have selected your fellow Levites from among the Israelites as a gift to you, dedicated to the LORD to do the work at the tent of meeting. ⁷ But only you and your sons may serve as priests in connection with everything at the altar and inside the curtain. I am giving you the service of the priesthood as a gift. Anyone else who comes near the sanctuary is to be put to death."

What is Hannukah?
also called the *Festival of Lights*

The traditional story is that during the rededication of the Second Temple in Jerusalem during the 2nd Century BC, there was an uprising against the Greeks and Syrians by the Maccabees, the Jewish Army. Story has it that they were down to their last oil and sent a soldier to get more oil for their lamps. The oil they had was expected to last no more than 1 day but lasted 8 days. There are 8 candles on the Menorah that is used during the annual festival of Hannukah. Hannukah translates as "dedication."

As each candle is lit the following prayer is recited:

Baruch atah Adonai Eloheinu Melech ha-olam, asher kid'shanu b-mitzvotav, v-tzivanu l'hadlik ner shel Hanukkah.

Blessed are you, Our God, Ruler of the Universe, who makes us holy through Your commandments, and commands us to light the Hanukkah lights.

Focus on Pastor Randy Bradley

I have always wanted to write a biography about Pastor Randy. He is one of those special people you meet once in a lifetime who is always kind and loving, no matter your own mood when you see him. I still see him occasionally at church on Sunday morning and he is one of those people I always want to say hello to.

I want to include him here since he played a major role in my journey and a special role in helping bring my older children their first understanding of God.

When my oldest child was old enough to attend Sunday school, we were already attending Independent Bible Church in Martinsburg, WV. The year was 2005. That year was the same year Pastor Randy Bradley took over Children's Ministries at the church. My son was in the kindergarten class and would grow up at IBC at least until he was 10 years old. It was also when he turned 10 that we left IBC for a hiatus, but we did come back after our youngest was born.

There was a time when Randy and his wife came to visit our home to talk about my son and his life at IBC but the reason for my focus here is about Randy himself and his style of communicating with children that has had a long-lasting impact on my own teaching styles and my own way of communicating with kids.

Randy and I are both tall. There was a time I remember him being much taller than me and I am pretty certain he is still at least ½ an inch taller in our older ages.

I am mentioning this because what Randy is so famous for in my memories is his ability to take his 6'3" frame and bend down low enough to speak eye to eye with children.

Every time I saw him speak to my children in classes, he would make sure he was speaking to them at their eye level. Never would I see him talk down to kids. There is a lot of deep thought you can put into this, and it is well worth it. Think about the way you speak to your own children. How is your relationship because of the way you speak to them. Do you ever try to speak to them at eye level? When sitting at the dinner table together it is pretty easy to do this but if you are talking to them when they are sitting on the floor in a classroom in Sunday school? Did you get down on the floor with them before you started to speak to them? Randy did this all the time. And I mean all the time.

It was only later in my own professional life when I became a teacher that I tried this. It amazed me very quickly how my impact on children was much more positive when I stopped talking down to them but rather went eye to eye with them. I always retain my authority as the teacher, but it is easier to keep them engaged when they can look at me without having to look up at the sky to see my face. I started sharing this with teachers at many schools in West Virginia and in Virginia. I called it the "Randy Bradley Teacher Strategy."

There is much more that can be said about Pastor Randy, but I will save this for my future biography of him, should I be so lucky to write it.

The Dreams

Sometime around my 10th birthday, soon after we moved into our new home, I started having dreams. Dreams that I remember to this day. I thank God, I don't still have them.

In my first dream I would wake up in the middle of the night and attempt to visit my parents in their bedroom. It is important to be able to visualize the second floor of the house. When you arrived at the top of the staircase the door to my parents' room was directly in front of you. If you were to turn right and look down at the hall, you would see a linen closet on the left side inside the stairwell to the 3rd floor. A couple of feet after the linen closet on the right side was a bathroom. Opposite the bathroom door was a short hallway to my sister's bedroom.

Directly in front of you would be the door to my bedroom. It was no more than 25 feet from my door to my parent's door.

841 Castlewood Terrace, Chicago 60640

In the dream I would start to walk down the hall but as I approached the linen closet, it was no longer there. In place of the linen closet was a brick fireplace with a red-hot blazing fire. Standing on the hearth in front of the fireplace was a family of human-like bears.

Unlike the family of bears in the fairy tale "Goldie Locks," these bears were far from friendly looking. My dreams got so bad that I would wake up and lay in my bed wide awake at night imagining that the bears were really in the hallway. I do not remember when I stopped fearing the bears but fortunately, I did.

My second dream, which was interspersed with the Bear dream involved the Devil. In this dream I would wake up and find myself in a large underground dungeon in a castle. If you saw the movie "Frankenstein" (1931 with Boris Karloff) you would have a clever idea of what I was imagining. In the middle of the dungeon was an enormous cauldron filled with boiling red lava. There were two metal staircases wrapped around the side of the cauldron, which met at a single point at the top. At the point that the two staircases came together was a metal platform about 5' x 5'.

In the middle of the platform stood the Devil. In my dream this Devil was bright red with a pitchfork and pointed tail. Every time I had this dream it would follow the same sequence. I would be in an extensive line of other children waiting to climb the stairwells. I would usually be about the 25th kid in line. The wait was always excruciating.

When I finally get the chance to climb the stairs, I would be darting my eyes left and right looking for my father, wondering where he was and if he would come to take me home. All the other children ahead of me would arrive at the top stairs and then as they stepped on the platform the Devil would take his fork and pitch them into the cauldron's boiling liquid. The climb took an eternity. My father would not show up until the very moment I arrived at the top stairs. He would then take my hand and we would go down another staircase leading to an ice cream shop.

It was always the A&W Ice Cream at the L Station on Lawrence Avenue in Chicago. When I was a kid, my father liked taking me for root beer floats at this particular location underneath the L tracks. Although unrelated we also went to a delicatessen in the Lawrence Hotel a couple of blocks east of the station.

When I would try to analyze this dream, I usually produced two explanations, but the "Devil" part of the dream never made sense unless it was just from movies I saw when I was younger. My father was away from home much of the time between my 8th and 12th birthdays. Perhaps another reason for the ice cream was being in the head-on collision when I was younger and lost most of my baby teeth. All I could eat was soft serve ice cream for weeks after the accident. As I mentioned above my father used to take me there.

Lawrence Avenue L Platform

The third dream started a bit later in my adolescence. I think the first time I had this dream was after I had turned 12 years old. This dream was much more sophisticated and mathematical. Now this was a Spiritual dream. The dream was a vision of two straight lines approaching one another but never connecting. Each time the ends would be ready to connect they would recede and continue their approach again. Once again, they would recede.

The backdrop for the lines was always empty space. When I tried to analyze this dream, I asked myself the same question which gave me as much anguish as the dream itself. "If there is a beginning to everything, what came before?" The headaches could get pretty severe.

I asked my mother for the answer to my questions. I do not remember if she ever offered me answers but if she did, they were never acceptable, and I continued to have the dreams.

I feared having the dreams since they always brought me great pains and suffering as a young person. I recall having these dreams in later years as an adult. I finally realized only recently, more than 30 years later, that it is not possible to answer this question without first having faith in the Lord and an infinite trust in our Creator.

I never had a recurrence of the dream after my spiritual awakening. I truly believe that the lines not connecting was a preview of my larger lingering question of my relationship with God. Like the times Pastor Mark would invite parishioners to accept Jesus and my inability to do so. My inability to stand up and walk downstairs from the balcony of the sanctuary is a good analogy of not being able to connect. His invitation was one side and my inability to accept was the other.

Photographs Index

Momo Taro	10
Goethe, Chicago	10
Chicago Snowstorm	13
Sinamaica, Venezuela	16
Cock Fight in Sinamaica	16
The House on Castlewood Terrace	17
Wallace Beery	18
Gloria Swanson	18
Studs Terkel	19
The Keystone Cops	20
Bob Hope	22
Bud Abbot & Lou Costello	24
The Edgewater Beach Hotel, Chicago	24
Tony Randall	25
Telly Savalas	26
Lucille Ball	26
Universal Studios	26
Dreidels and Hannukah Geld	27
Hannukah Menorah	29
Ethical Humanist Society Billboard	31
Anshe Emet Hebrew Day School, Chicago	42
Snake Charmer	47
Taj Mahal, India	48
Holocaust Victims, Jerusalem Holocaust Museum	53
Wailing Wall, Jerusalem	55
Senn High School, Chicago	59
St. John's Military Academy Main Entrance	65
SJMA Delta Company Main Drag	68
Harand Camp, Elkhart Lake, Wisconsin	69
SJMA Victory Memorial Chapel	70
SGM William Golden	71

Caricature	**71**
Chaim Potok	**82**
Independent Bible Church logo	**101**
Independent Bible Church, Martinsburg, WV	**102**
IBC Praise Team	**103**
Pastor Mark Johnson	**104**
Pastor George Michael	**105**
The IBC Sanctuary and The Balcony	**110**
Pastor Curt Lowry	**124**
Pastor Randy Bradley	**133**
841 Castlewood Terrace, Chicago	**138**
Lawrence St. "L" Station, Chicago	**142**

Made in the USA
Columbia, SC
10 April 2025